Photoshop CC
For Beginners:

The Ultimate Digital Photography and Photo Editing Tips and Tricks Guide For Creating Amazing Photos

By

Joseph Joyner

Table of Contents

Photoshop CC For Beginners: The Ultimate Digital Photography and Photo Editing Tips and Tricks Guide For Creating Amazing Photos

By Joseph Joyner

Introduction

The world of photography has become a better place ever since the release of Photoshop tool which is flourishing with emblazoning ease throughout the world. Many refreshing ideas from developers met the fundamental needs of photographers ranging from amateurs to professionals who always felt something is lagging in their photographs. For fulfilling such requirements the basic version flowed with multiple options which for a time period satisfied one and all. However, as the evolution of technology takes place in rapid succession, users realized certain drawbacks and the designers ever since coped up with expectations and are constantly upgrading their application. The new Photoshop CC is the latest version from the developers, which promise more efficiency, effects and a touch of "cloud" magic. Let us have a look into the world's most preferred photo editing tool, i.e., Photoshop CC to understand the variety of new features added and how the new version increased its proficiency in editing images.

John Knoll and Thomas were the two people who created this amazing photo editing tool, Photoshop. It is not just a photo editing tool; in fact, you can call it as an amazing tool to do magic with the images. This was created in the year 1988 and since then this tool has gained a lot of popularity.

Let us begin this book about Photoshop CC with an introduction to the interface and a few important terms that every Photoshop user should know. This is going to make working with Photoshop easier and simple for you as a Photoshop user.

Chapter 1. The Best Cameras to Use for Digital Photography and Further Editing

When you are using Photoshop CC for editing and adding new effects to the photos, you will have to use the RAW images that are clicked using your digital camera. The RAW images will not be detected by the computer, and hence you will have to convert them into such form that can be recognized by the computer like .JPEG or TIFF files. Every digital camera will have its own software for converting the photograph into the desirable formats that can be recognized by the computer. You should be very careful while applying any kind of effect to the images, but that can be done only when the quality of the images is really good. So, here are a few features of digital camera that you should check before you buy digital camera that is best to use for digital photography and for further editing.

1. When you want the quality of the RAW photographs to be high, then you should make sure that the resolution is high. But along with resolution, you will have to take care of the sensor and lens quality as well. For example, you should always choose an 8 megapixel

digital camera with good sensor and lens than a 10 mega pixel digital camera with a small lens.

2. Color reproduction is another important feature that you will have to take care of. A camera that is able to record the real life colors is more important.

3. Manual focusing is also an important feature that you should take care of. When you are checking the digital cameras at the store, you will find that almost all the cameras that you have seen so far are having the auto focus feature, but you will be able to see just a few with manual focusing and that is very important. Manual focusing is very important because you will be able to decide where exactly to focus for obtaining impeccable photographs.

4. Stability of the image is also something that you need to check carefully. Many images even when clicked with a lot of care will be slightly blurry and that is due to the dimness of the surroundings or the use of zoom too much. Some cameras have an image stabilization feature and that can help you in improving the image quality.

5. When you are buying a digital camera make sure that the lens settings should be low and the zoom should be as high as possible.

Chapter 2. How to Use Photoshop CC Effectively

Photoshop CC or Photoshop Creative Cloud has become a boon for all those people who work on Photoshop. There are so many interesting features added to the Photoshop CC like retouch tools and Smart object's expanded support. Photoshop CC can be used for making much more with your photos like you can do touch up to your photos; you can add many interesting and high quality graphics to the images. If you are using Photoshop CC for the first time, then it is going to be little complicated for understanding and using the interface of Photoshop.

Chapter 3. How to Crop Images

Cropping the image in Photoshop CC is something that is done too often. You may want to crop your image for many reasons like you may feel that the image is having a lot of space around the main subject, and that can happen even when the quality of the image is too good. You may also like to crop the image, when you want to resize the image like increasing or decreasing the size of a particular object in the image.

1. For cropping the image, you will first have to open the image and make sure that the quality of the image is really good. Any photo that is being used in Photoshop CC for applying any kind of effects should be of high quality, so that the image is going to be best or natural even after editing. Now, after you open the image, select the crop tool from the Photoshop toolbar. You can now use the crop area that is being shown to you on your image or you can choose to change the cropping area as well. If you want to change it, then you will have to drag the corners of the crop area that is being shown to you.

2. You have a control bar for cropping your images and if you have a specific requirement for the cropping like if you are aware of the dimensions that you need, then you can make sure of this option. There are a number of options available for you in the control bar and you can choose the one according to your requirement.

3. You can choose overlay guides which can help you in cropping in a better way. There are many overlay guides options and you can choose one of your choices or you can even choose not to apply overlays as well. After cropping the image, you may want to remove the area outside the cropped area, and in that case you will have to select the DELETE CROPPED PIXELS, and if that button is not selected, then the pixels will still remain. In case, you want a different area of the image that you deleted, then you can go for it.

4. Straightening your image is another interesting feature that you can apply while you are cropping images. If you have clicked the image of something and that is looking slightly tilted, then you can straighten it by drawing a straight line on the image and then make it straight. Once everything is done, have a look at the

image and if you are happy, then you can apply the crop and save it.

Here are a few interesting things that you can do by using Crop:-

1. Cropping and rotation can be done at the same time. Generally, when you are cropping, you will have to hold the mouse button and when you want to rotate, you will have to leave the button and then rotate. But if you are double clicking the image and then cropping it, you can even rotate the image at the same time. This is something that is less known to people, but you can definitely try it out.

2. Did you try perspective cropping anytime? Normally, when you drag the marquee on the image, then you can free the mouse button. Now, at the top select the perspective check box. When this check box is selected, then you will be able to drag each corner of the image individually.

3. The cropped area need not be deleted completely. You can place the crop marquee on the image and then select the hide button, which is below the menu bar. Now, the cropped area will not be visible if you

double click on the image. But that does not mean that it is deleted. It is just hidden and you can still use it when required.

4. Preset cropping is another interesting feature that many people miss when they are using crop tool for the first time. You will have many predefined preset options to choose. So you can select one of those preset options that are available or you can choose to create your own. You can save your preset cropping preferences and they will be saved for use at a later time.

Chapter 4. How to Work with Shades and Colors

When you are using the images or the photos while designing websites, then you will sometimes feel that the color of the images are not as per the requirement. That means, they will not be suitable for the website that you are designing or the background of the image does not match along with the image. Using Photoshop, you will be able to change the colors and shades in the image and that is going to make them just perfect for your requirements.

1. Here is a small example about how to apply a different color to the image parts or how to change the color. You will first have to open that image or the photo that you think does not match with your requirements. You will also have to create a new layer and open the image and that is called as the background layer. You have the new layer create icon at the bottom right of the screen. Once these two are opened, you should check whether the background layer is selected or not. Before you do anything with

the image, you will have to check the PATHS option on the top left corner.

2. Once you are done with this, now it is time to select the pen from your tool box and start marking the area that you want to change the color. When you are selecting the area, make sure that the loops are connected well. Once the selection is done, you will now have to right click on that selected area and select MARK SELECTION. This is going to pop up a new window for you and you will have to select the feather value. It has to be either one or two. If you are thinking you have selected the area almost right, then make it one, otherwise if it is beyond, then you will have to make this value as 2. Then select OK.

3. Once the selection process is done completely, then you see that the area that you selected is blinking. Once it starts blinking, then it is time for you to remove the color from that part. For removing color, go to the IMAGE tab and ADJUSTMENT and in that drop down select DESATURATE. Now, you should not deselect the area that you selected in the background layers, and at the same time select the new layer that you created at the beginning and select color picker. You should now

select the color with which you want to replace the original color. You should select the paint bucket and you will have to fill the area that you selected. For example, if you want to apply to both the eyes, then you should make sure that you are selecting the two eyes, so that when you are applying to one eye, then it would be applied to both the eyes. You should now deselect the selected area. You can you the same process for applying the effect like changing the color. You can select any part of the image or you can select the different parts of the face like eyes, ears, lips and the skin tone as well. It is very simple to apply the colors or recolor any part of the image. You can do it for the whole image and that is going to enhance the look of the image.

4. This is one of the simplest ways to change the color and you will not need too much of the experience of doing it. But you will need to be very careful while selecting the image that needs color change. Also make sure that while you are selecting the color for replacement, you are not deselecting the area that you selected for making color changes, otherwise you will have to do the entire thing once again. You will get perfect as you keep doing it. While replacing the color,

choosing the right color is also important to make sure that your edited image looks original and natural.

Chapter 5. Improving Quality & Highlighting The Faces in The Picture

Compared to the older versions of Photoshop, the latest version of Creative Cloud had come up with brilliant new features which allow us to enrich the quality of a photograph. Among them improving picture quality and highlighting the faces in the picture is an important one. Photoshop CC has more advanced features like the expanded smart object support, improved 3D painting, editable rounded rectangles, multi-shape, and path selection. These features will ensure to rejuvenate those photographs which appear dull and lifeless resulting in spirited photographs which look bright and attractive.

The process of picture editing involves simple steps mentioned below:

1. The foremost step is to enlarge the image to the extreme, where the user can comprehend every part of the picture. This enables to have a microscopic view at every minute detail available in the image, further resulting in analysis of errors.

2. or prevention of jaggy appearance during high enhancement, anti-aliasing option will help and gives smoother appearance.

3. Present day Photoshop users won't go beyond RGB or CMYK. This version has much advanced feature called as Lab color which helps in shifting the colors of the actual image. One can find a dramatic change in the image after using this tool.

4. Gaussian Blur helps in making the edges of the image crisper than they appear. This will enrich the quality of the faces in the picture a bit further. This particular feature will highlight the faces in the given image.

By following the above mentioned steps with utmost patience fruitful results can be obtained. However, it also depends on user's creativity to make a simple photograph evolve into an excellent one. In addition to these swapping enhances to merge images if it is needed. Any other further improvement has to be done with a simple brush tool which is not that difficult.

Chapter 6. Measures to Be Followed While Creating Black and White Photographs

Modern pictures contain many colors which make it attractive; however black and white pictures are always unique. This is the reason many people still prefer to have photographs in black and white. Technically the tool used for conversion of colored pictures to black and white is called as gray scale. By careful application of gray scale and taking good measures during color conversion realistic and adorable black and white pictures can be obtained.

Here we are going to learn about the various tools used in gray scale imaging and the measures to be taken while using this tool. Gray scale editing mainly relies on the contrast of the image along with filters. However, it is easy to convert a colored image to grayscale, but to get the optimal results one needs to work on the most efficient options available within gray scale and needs to get highly creative.

To make any kind of conversion go to image option, choose adjustments from the drop down menu followed by black and white option. Select the adjustment layer icon which is present in the layers panel. You can see a new panel, which has a sliding control. There you can make changes in the brightness among various colors.

First measure to follow is selecting the best subject for photography. It is a must which can enhance your image through Photoshop effects. Few backgrounds bring bad effects to the image after grayscale conversion. So while capturing a picture, considering the contrast, shape and form are the major principles without which the formula will not succeed. It's necessary to pay attention to these details. Texture is another important aspect for these pictures. For instance; clouds, pebbles and so on can bring interesting effects in any black and white picture. Graphic composition is one of the most important things to consider. Take care of the features in the scene positioned across the frame.

Few subjects give bad impact in your black and white images like bland skies. Choose a good subject that elevates your black and white images in Photoshop.

Filters play an amazing role in color conversion:

In Photoshop CC smart filters are the best choice to make professional effects to the image. But it's tough to deal with them as a beginner. Among them, there are few essential (most used) tools which will be useful for black and white image conversion and enhancement.

1. Darkening a blue sky is one of the popular methods followed in any gray scale image conversion. And it's quite easy to make. A high contrast Red filter is used to make changes. It can create a high contrast image.

2. Using blue filter over the image brightens the blue and darkens the yellow.

3. The green filter produces a remarkable lower contrast image.

Chapter 7. Correction of Unwanted Elements Using Photoshop CC

Removing unwanted elements or defects from an image is done by using the fill and patch tools. Let's see how these two will work in a step –wise procedure:

Removing objects using Fill tool:

1. Select an image like a light post for which you want to make the change. Open it with a medium to large sized object (it depends upon the type of document you are working on). Single-layered document is always suggestible for a new learner. This document has to be duplicated by using Ctrl-J.

2. Pressing Shift-W will show an icon in the Toolbox which has to be activated. Now, turn on the Auto-Enhance checkbox which will be found in the Options Bar. This helps in selecting the particular image precisely and perfectly.

3. The light post which is to be painted is selected. While you paint it adds same colored pixels upon the selected portion. There will be a problem if we select more portion of the background.

4. In order to introduce more pixels we need to expand the selection. Anyhow, you are working on a small image; you need to enter around 8 to 20 pixels into the selected portion.

5. 'Content-Aware' is selected from the Use menu after choosing Fill from Edit menu. Just by clicking OK the selected portion will be filled with surrounding pixels and converts them. The special feature of voodoo used by it will make the necessary requirements to the selected portion. Once you succeed in this you will get a lot of space to enter your text if needed.

Removing objects using Patch tool:

1. Pressing Shift-Ctrl-N will create a new layer upon the selected image. Give a suitable name and simply click OK button.

2. Pressing Shift-j repeatedly will enable an icon to appear in the Toolbox only after activating the Patch tool. Turn on the Sample All Layers checkbox from the Patch drop-down menu. Remember that you shouldn't change the Adaptation drop-down menu.

3. Select the area you want to make changes by simply click-and-drag method. You can extend the area to insert more pixels in the background.

4. The area you want to fix has to be dragged out of the image. A preview will be shown on how the image will look like after the changes are made.

5. To know how much changes had been done to the image can be seen in the Adaptation drop-down menu present in the Options Bar.

Chapter 8. Main Differences Between Photoshop CS6 and Photoshop CC

For a new user interested in photo editing or experienced image editors, it is suggestible to know the difference between older versions of Adobe Photoshop and the newer versions. This would enable the user to precisely understand why there is a new version and the addition of essential features which sets apart both the versions. Photoshop cs6 is the previous version of Adobe Photoshop which has been replaced by Creative Cloud version.

It is needless to say, whenever a new version is released into the market curiosity among the people increases as to what the new features available are. Photoshop CC contains all the tool applications found in Photoshop cs6, hence Adobe announced that there won't be any further releases of Creative Suit. The following variations differentiate Photoshop cs6 and Photoshop CC.

1. The major difference is that Photoshop cs6 does not allow the user to work on the internet. In contrast, Photoshop CC contains creative cloud function which

enables the user to work directly on the internet, further enabling him/her to share the live projects with people across the world without ever leaving the tool. In addition, this service is provided by a mere registration in Creative Cloud organization which is not a strenuous task by any means.

2. The integration with Adobe Stock photos is a considerable difference between two versions, as finding stock photos is very difficult and every photo editing individual is well aware of this fact. Adobe Stock provides over 40 million photos which certainly will ensure novelty to the user. Furthermore, the cost efficiency increases because purchasing single stock photos can really burn the income of the user. For creative needs this is the best feature as the user need not go elsewhere for finding new images for the creation of new designs.

3. As there will be no future Creative Suit versions released, cs6 is the last of its kind. On the contrary, Creative Cloud is compatible with all future updates which can benefit the user to maintain a constant relationship with Adobe.

4. Photoshop cs6 came with an annual membership option which declined the chance for updates during this period without loss of money. Adobe recognized the inconvenience by such long membership options. Therefore, CC is released with monthly payment options at affordable prices. In addition, for those users who need specific applications in a complete Photoshop CC package, there is an option to buy the desired application for considerably small amounts.

5. One of the most interesting features of Photoshop CC which is absent in Photoshop cs6 is the presence of 3D printing support. It may seem off the chart technology, but Adobe through sincere efforts has made it possible for Photoshop CC to allow 3D printing of any image processed through the tool. Although this technology requires the use of 3D printers, it is not so hard to find these devices nowadays.

Apart from these, there are many unique features which distinguish Photoshop CC from Photoshop cs6. The following are a few exclusive features introduced in Photoshop CC:

Adobe camera raw 9 and camera raw as a filter, camera shake reduction, real-time healing brush, blur gallery motion effects and additive noise, windows HiDPI (High dots per inch) support, Adobe generator smart sharpen, improved windows 8.1 touch and stylus support, perspective warp, focus mask, desktop fonts from Adobe type kit, multiple instances of layer styles, glyph panel, etc. In addition to these essential features there are many minor changes and upgrades which do not need mention. Furthermore, many update trials from Photoshop cs6 to CC resulted in numerous improvements which are all included in Photoshop CC.

Conclusion

In conclusion, any new enthusiast has to know that a simple download of the Photoshop CC is not sufficient. It is of prior importance to be knowledgeable about every aspect of this wondrous editing tool. The user must be capable of understanding every feature offered by the new version to completely enjoy the benefits it provides. The ease with which the above mentioned tasks can be achieved alone makes Photoshop CC admirable and beyond compare in the field of photo editing. By effective application of this splendid editing tool, the user without any strain can obtain desired results in no time, and can share with anyone in the world. With regards to competition, there is no other editing tool in the market capable of outrunning the latest version and the case may remain the same for several decades. Hence, one can reliably state that "Photoshop CC is the best there is in the market".

Thank You Page

I want to personally thank you for reading my book. I hope you found information in this book useful and I would be very grateful if you could leave your honest review about this book. I certainly want to thank you in advance for doing this.

If you have the time, you can check my other books too.